Original title:

The Essence of Us

Author: Scott Parker

ISBN HARDBACK: 978-9908-0-1072-4

ISBN PAPERBACK: 978-9908-0-1073-1

The Space Between Us

In the gaps where laughter hides,
We trip on jokes and silly rides.
Frog on a log, they try to stay,
But slip and slide, oh what a day!

With quirks that dance in silly steps,
Like clumsy ducks, with no preps.
We poke at hearts, we tease with glee,
In this crazy space, just you and me.

Blossoming Together

Two odd blooms in the garden plot,
We bloom like carrots, not quite hot.
With petals that twist in awkward grace,
We giggle through each colorful space.

Sunshine and rain – oh, what a mix!
We dance in mud with our funny tricks.
Together we grow, not perfect but bright,
Sprouting our joy, a beautiful sight!

Petals of Connection

Fallen petals on a busy street,
Connecting hearts with every beat.
A dance of colors, all in a swirl,
Like jellybeans tossed in a world.

Each petal tells tales of clumsy cheer,
Spinning stories that tickle the ear.
Between the laughs, we find our tune,
Under the glow of a funny moon.

Collage of Us

In a scrapbook filled with silly quirks,
We paste our moments, and where it works.
Doodles of humor in a haphazard style,
Creating a patchwork that makes us smile.

So glue those giggles, stick them tight,
With memories that sparkle, oh what a sight!
We're a collage, a beautiful mess,
In the gallery of life, we laugh, we bless.

Tides of Affection

You spilled your coffee on my shoe,
I laughed so hard, thought you were blue.
Our sticky laughs, like gum on toes,
In this wild sea, affection flows.

You dance like nobody's watching near,
While I pretend I'm a pioneer.
In waves of giggles, we find our way,
Riding the tides come what may.

Ties that Bind

You stole my fries, that cheeky grin,
I rolled my eyes, but where do I begin?
With jokes and jests, like neon lights,
You pull me in on the funniest nights.

Your socks don't match, it's quite a sight,
We laugh, we roll, and hold on tight.
These silly moments, woven fine,
In this crazy quilt, we intertwine.

Symphony of Hearts

You sing off-key, but it's my jam,
Each note a laugh, oh, what a sham!
In this orchestra of silly sounds,
Joy in the chaos, sweet love abounds.

With spoons as drums, we rock the place,
Every silly dance, a warm embrace.
Together we blend like ice cream swirls,
A funky tune, our hearts unfurl.

Celestial Interlinking

You tripped on stars, I caught the fall,
In this galactic dance, we have a ball.
With laughter loud like a comet's tail,
    Together we sail, we never fail.

Our misfit dreams are cosmic dust,
In this great void, it's always a must.
With every slip, we sparkle and shine,
In our universe, your light is mine.

Shadows Dancing

Our shadows prance in silly glee,
Twisting shapes that no one can see.
We leap and bound, a joyful game,
Laughing loudly, never the same.

In the moonlight, we twirl around,
Like clumsy dancers on shaky ground.
With every step, we trip and fall,
Yet still we rise, ignoring it all.

Celestial Interlinking

You tripped on stars, I caught the fall,
In this galactic dance, we have a ball.
With laughter loud like a comet's tail,
Together we sail, we never fail.

Our misfit dreams are cosmic dust,
In this great void, it's always a must.
With every slip, we sparkle and shine,
In our universe, your light is mine.

Shadows Dancing

Our shadows prance in silly glee,
Twisting shapes that no one can see.
We leap and bound, a joyful game,
Laughing loudly, never the same.

In the moonlight, we twirl around,
Like clumsy dancers on shaky ground.
With every step, we trip and fall,
Yet still we rise, ignoring it all.

Under One Canopy

Beneath this tree, our laughter flies,
With squirrel friends and endless pies.
The branches sway, they seem to hum,
While we feast on cake and bubblegum.

Sunlight tickles, keeps us warm,
We dodge the raindrops, that's our charm.
A game of who can shout the loudest,
We're the very best—there's none that doubt us!

Heartstrings Unplugged

Our tunes are loud, a glorious mess,
With off-key notes, we still impress.
When one hits flat, the other will grin,
For in our flops, the fun begins.

With air guitars, we rock the floor,
Pretending to be stars, we want more!
Our inner band, a comical crew,
Made up of hearts that always stay true.

Colors of Our Harmony

Splashes of orange, blue, and green,
We paint our world, it's quite the scene.
With mismatched socks and hats too bright,
We strut our colors, a joyful sight.

Each brushstroke tells a quirky tale,
Of rainy days and epic fails.
Together we laugh, we scribble and play,
In this canvas of life, we'll forever stay.

Tapestry of Souls

We're tangled threads, what a sight!
Stitching quirks both day and night.
Your sock is missing, my shoe's stolen,
Yet laughter blooms, our hearts are golden.

A mishap here, a slip up there,
In our world, no room for despair.
With every snort, with every sigh,
We weave a joy that never runs dry.

Reflections in the Mirror of You

In mirrors' gaze, I see your grin,
We look so off, but still, we win.
The hair's a mess, the outfit's grand,
Together, reigns this fun-filled land.

You nick my fries, I steal your drink,
In this crazy dance, we think and blink.
Our faces read like a comic book,
With every page, a laugh we took.

Unspoken Bond

We speak in looks, in silly poses,
Like winding paths through thorny roses.
You raise an eyebrow, I roll my eyes,
Together, we cook up wild surprise.

Our inside jokes, a secret choir,
Sing silly tunes that never tire.
A nudge, a wink, we crack the code,
With every laugh, our friendship glowed.

Journey of Two

With mismatched socks, we hit the road,
A quirky van, our laughter flowed.
Map's upside down, but who's in charge?
On this wild ride, the fun is large.

Through bumps and turns, our joy won't fade,
Life's a circus where jokes paraded.
With you beside me, come what may,
Every twist brings a brighter day.

Our Silent Conversations

In the corner, you wink, I grin,
A whole chat, without a din.
You shake your head, mime a frown,
While I pretend to wear a crown.

From nods that speak of pizza dreams,
To goofy grins and silly schemes.
Our eyes converse, and hearts collide,
In quiet laughter, we confide.

Fusion of Spirits

You like chocolate, I love pie,
Mix them both? Oh, let's not try!
But in our dance, two steps we take,
A cocktail blend that's sure to shake.

Your quirks, my laughs, they intertwine,
Like peanut butter on a vine.
We stir together, joy and glee,
In our mad mix, we both agree.

Paths Converging

Two paths meet at a roadside stall,
You want ice cream; I'll have it all!
Trip over giggles, stumble on spry,
  Feathered confetti fills the sky.

With every step, we tease and jest,
 Side by side, we think we're best.
 As life leads us, come what may,
We'll walk together, come what day.

Celestial Manifestations

The stars above are blinking bright,
You nudge me; it's a funny sight!
'Is that a comet or your shoe?'
As laughter floats on midnight blue.

Cosmic jokes in the Milky Way,
You say "aliens!" when I sway.
Our giggles echo through the night,
In the cosmos, we find delight.

Unity in Diversity

In a world of mismatched socks,
We laugh at our quirks and knocks.
With ice cream flavors far and wide,
Together we take life in stride.

Frogs in top hats, cats on bikes,
We find our joy in silly hikes.
Sing a song of silly things,
As each of us with laughter sings.

Fragments of Forever

A puzzle with pieces askew,
Who knew that toast could be blue?
Time slips as we giggle and play,
Collecting memories like a bouquet.

Our quirky past, a jumbled mess,
Yet in our chaos, we find success.
With each tale, we grow a bit bolder,
Caught between laughter, we get older.

Dance of Shared Dreams

In mismatched shoes we twirl and spin,
The floor may wobble, but we're all in.
With laughter as the beat of our hearts,
We dance through life, playing our parts.

We tango with our silly flaws,
Jumbling our feet with applause.
The rhythm of joy is our guide,
As we twirl together with pride.

Mosaic of Moments

Life's a patchwork of random bits,
Like socks worn with quirky knits.
Stitching the laughs into our days,
In colors that twist and amaze.

With every mistake, a gem we find,
In mishaps we're perfectly aligned.
Together we craft a vibrant show,
In this silly life, we steal the glow.

A Symphony of Hearts

Our laughter dances in the air,
Like socks misplaced, a playful pair.
Music in our silly chatter,
A symphony where giggles scatter.

You steal my fries, I take your drink,
Together we make the stars blink.
With every joke, we twist and sway,
In this grand band, we both play.

Threads Woven in Time

Each moment shared, a quirky thread,
Like mismatched shoes, we both tread.
Our stories sewn with laughter bright,
A tapestry of silly delight.

Through tangled tales and frosty air,
We sew our joy, a perfect pair.
With every stitch, a tale we weave,
In this cloth of fun, we believe.

Through the Window of Us

Peeking out, we start to grin,
At goofy memes and silly spins.
Through our glass, the world's a joke,
A quirky place that makes us poke.

We laugh at clouds shaped like a cat,
While dancing to that silly bat.
Through the panes of our shared view,
Life's a stage, just me and you.

Cherished Moments

A spilled drink, a snorty laugh,
Little quirks that make us half.
In every blunder, joy shines through,
Those cherished times, just me and you.

From midnight talks to cheesy snacks,
We calculate our silly hacks.
In these moments, pure delight,
A treasure chest, our hearts are bright.

Tidal Waves of Affection

When we splash in laughter's sea,
You steal my fries, oh woe is me!
With silly grins and playful jabs,
We ride each wave, no time for drabs.

In puddles we jump, no care to fall,
Your goofy dance, it says it all.
Bouncing like dolphins, we twist and spin,
In this chaotic ocean, we always win.

Reflections of Our Journey

We took the bus that went off-track,
And ended up with a snack attack.
Maps upside down, a giggle parade,
Every wrong turn, a fun escapade.

Our photos are blurry, faces all mashed,
But every snapshot is joyfully hashed.
We dance through the past with silly flair,
In this scrapbook life, nothing could compare.

The Language of Us

We speak in puns and winks so sly,
With a wink and a nudge, we'd both start to fly.
Inside jokes bloom like flowers in spring,
Our laughter's the song that makes our hearts sing.

Your snorts and my giggles create quite the tune,
We laugh at the stars, we sing to the moon.
An unspoken bond, a funny embrace,
In this comic dance, we've found our place.

Fragmented Stories

We once had a plan to bake a great pie,
But flour-filled faces made us laugh till we cry.
Eggs on the ceiling and sprinkles galore,
Our kitchen's a circus, oh, what a chore!

Tales that get tangled, like yarn on the floor,
We stitch them together, then burst out in more.
With each silly chapter, we create quite the mess,
But in every mishap, we're truly blessed.

Whole Heart

You stole my heart, but hey, who's counting?
Your jokes are like gold, always mountains of routing.
Our quirks and our giggles, they band together tight,
In this silly journey, we're a pure delight.

With a heart that is whole, made of chuckles and quirks,
We dance in the chaos, where laughter works.
So here's to our madness, let's give it a toast,
In the grand scheme of life, you're what I love most.

Fragmented Stories

We once had a plan to bake a great pie,
But flour-filled faces made us laugh till we cry.
Eggs on the ceiling and sprinkles galore,
Our kitchen's a circus, oh, what a chore!

Tales that get tangled, like yarn on the floor,
We stitch them together, then burst out in more.
With each silly chapter, we create quite the mess,
But in every mishap, we're truly blessed.

Whole Heart

You stole my heart, but hey, who's counting?
Your jokes are like gold, always mountains of routing.
Our quirks and our giggles, they band together tight,
In this silly journey, we're a pure delight.

With a heart that is whole, made of chuckles and quirks,
We dance in the chaos, where laughter works.
So here's to our madness, let's give it a toast,
In the grand scheme of life, you're what I love most.

Entangled in Time

When clocks tick loud in silly sync,
We argue over cups and drinks,
Your shoe's a smile, my values shift,
Together we create a cosmic rift.

In tangled hair and quirky socks,
We dance around like two feathered flocks,
A toast to all the times we stray,
And laugh our worries all away.

With every bite of random cake,
You tease my love for peanut flake,
In moments loud and others shy,
We chase the time, oh my, oh my!

So here's to clocks that spin so fast,
To silly jokes that never last,
In funny fits of friendship's cheer,
We find the best in every year.

Moments Crafting Memories

Each second wraps a joyous jest,
In wild adventures, we're the best,
With crumbs of laughter lost in bread,
We forge our path by what we said.

From spilled drinks to quirky bloopers,
Our life's a series of silly troopers,
With little giggles echoing loud,
In our quirky world, we're so proud.

We capture time in snapshots sweet,
With wobbly grins and dancing feet,
The mementos of our goofy chase,
Are treasures tucked in heart's embrace.

So let's create some more today,
Forget the serious, come what may,
In every moment, let's find delight,
Like fireflies dancing in the night.

Whirlwinds of Connection

In swirling winds of playful glee,
We spin and twirl, just you and me,
Our laughter floats like cotton candy,
With every twist, we get more randy.

While chaos rains and plans go skewed,
We turn the mess into a mood,
With silly faces, we embrace the storm,
Making every wrong feel just as warm.

The whirlwinds of our wildest dreams,
Are stitched together with bright seams,
In friendship's fabric, cozy threads,
We craft a life where humor spreads.

So when the skies begin to pout,
We'll dance in puddles, laugh it out,
In every gust, a memory flies,
Like butterflies beneath the skies.

Silhouettes of Together

In shadowed forms, we find our groove,
With silly dances, watch us move,
Your goofy grin, my rolling eyes,
In our own world, we win the prize.

Like sketches drawn in midnight ink,
Our stories blend, we pause to think,
With every quirk and midnight snack,
We craft the maps we won't look back.

Our silhouettes in sunset hues,
Dance on walls like playful muse,
In whispered jokes and secret tales,
We navigate with laughter's sails.

So here's to us, two meddling fools,
In a world that often breaks the rules,
Together etched, in moments bright,
A sunrise painted with pure delight.

Blossoms of Shared Dreams

In a garden where we play,
Laughter sprinkles, bright as day.
We plant our hopes, a quirky mix,
With socks on hands, we craft our tricks.

Petals dance in silly ways,
We chase them down through sunny rays.
With every giggle, seeds we sow,
In this wild patch, our dreams will grow.

Bumblebees join in our cheer,
Spinning tales they lend an ear.
Together we create a scene,
A festival of what we mean.

So let the blossoms boldly bloom,
In our shared garden, there's always room.
With each new sprout and laugh that's shared,
Life's a canvas, with love declared.

Infinite Currents

Like rivers flowing side by side,
We make waves with every stride.
Splashing joy as we collide,
In this dance, there's no place to hide.

We paddle boats made of bright dreams,
Rowing hard, or so it seems.
But when we laugh, the burdens glide,
Through the twists of life, we take the ride.

Fish join in with chirpy chatter,
Bubble-blowing makes us scatter.
With each little ripple and jest,
Together we conquer this quirky quest.

So here we sail, just you and me,
Through waves of giggles, wild and free.
With oars of humor, we'll chart the course,
In this river, we find our force.

Portrait of Our Union

In the morning light, I see your face,
Hair a mess, but full of grace.
You steal the sheets, oh what a treat,
Your sleepy smile makes life complete.

We argue over who controls the TV,
You laugh at shows, while I just flee.
A thousand bickering, a shared delight,
Our love's a sitcom, day and night.

You keep the socks, I lose the keys,
A chaos whirling, oh how it frees!
In mismatched shoes, we strut about,
Forever laughing, there's no doubt.

When life throws curveballs, we just grin,
Our joke-telling games, they'll never thin.
A portrait drawn with colors bright,
Together we bloom, a funny sight!

Harmonies of Two Souls

In a kitchen, pots go clank,
You say my cooking's got a prank.
I add a dash of love, you see,
How did it turn to mystery?

We dance around the living room,
You step on toes, but I don't fume.
With giggles echoing in the air,
We spin like crazy without a care.

The cat watches with a disdain,
As we both sing in perfect vain.
Our off-key notes fill every nook,
A symphony of jest, not a book.

At times you wear my favorite hat,
Look like a clown, but I love that!
Our laughter's worth a million bucks,
Together, oh my, what funny luck!

Whirls of Together

Round and round, we spin with glee,
In a whirlwind, just you and me.
We twirl through clouds of cotton candy,
Mixing up fun, oh so dandy!

With rainbow socks and silly shoes,
We leap and laugh, there's never blues.
In this circus, we're the stars,
Juggling dreams under bright guitars.

As the wind plays in our hair,
Caught in giggles everywhere.
We dance through chaos, no time to rest,
This silly ride is simply the best!

So grab my hand, let's spin some more,
In this whirls of joy, we rock the floor.
Together, we'll weave laughter's thread,
In this tapestry of fun, we're led.

The Bridge We Build

Two sides meet at this fine place,
With silly hats and an odd brace.
We hammer joy, we nail down fun,
Together we shine, like the sun!

Planks of laughter, beams of glee,
We wave at ourselves in the sea.
With every step, we trip and roll,
But with you here, I feel so whole.

A bridge of quirks and playful tunes,
We chase the stars and dance with moons.
Falling down, then jumping high,
In this wacky world, we'll never die.

So let's construct more wobbly spans,
With humor's glue and warm, wide hands.
In each mistake, a memory made,
Through this bridge, our laughter won't fade.

An Intricate Dance

With two left feet, you try to sway,
I laugh aloud, you push away.
Yet in this shuffle, hand in hand,
We find the rhythm, understand.

You trip on air, a glorious fall,
Laughter erupts — you heed my call.
Our goofy spins, a twirl so grand,
In this crazy world, we take a stand.

When one says 'no,' the other will cheer,
Your taste for cheese, I hold so dear.
In mismatched tunes, we choose to groove,
Together forever, we always move.

With every dip, our quirks collide,
In this funny waltz, we take great pride.
The world's our stage, so let us twirl,
My partner in dance, my perfect whirl!

Beneath the Same Stars

Under the night sky, we lay wide-eyed,
You point at planets, am I the guide?
With your theories that twist and bend,
We argue 'till laughter is our best friend.

I swear I saw a UFO fly,
You laugh and say, 'That's just the pie.'
We eat the dessert under cosmic beams,
Even the stars join in our dreams.

The constellations seem to agree,
Our quirky love is wild and free.
In every laugh and silly jest,
We find our peace; this life's the best.

So here we lie, in this cosmic sea,
Two shooting stars, wild as can be.
In our universe, full of play,
Together forever, come what may!

In the Heart's Embrace

In laughter wrapped, our quirks unfold,
Like socks mismatched, a tale retold.
Your silly dance, my chuckle loud,
Together we stand, a merry crowd.

Like pancakes flipped, we rise and fall,
With syrup dreams, we heed the call.
A shared pizza slice, two forks collide,
In every bite, our joy is wide.

When life throws pies, we duck and weave,
Each crumb a tale that we'll believe.
In goofy gifs and tales that stray,
Our hearts compose a jesting play.

Embraced in fun, we do not hide,
With silly hats, we mock the tide.
A friendship forged in humor's flame,
In the heart's embrace, we'll stake our claim.

Echoes of Unity

When we laugh loud, echoes align,
Like jokes shared over sips of wine.
Your punchline hits, my giggle's dear,
In this duet, we conquer fear.

We share our dreams like awful puns,
Each quirky thought like goofy runs.
In every whim, a voice that's true,
Together, we bring light anew.

With memes exchanged, we spark delight,
In playful banter, we take flight.
Our voices dance, a silly tune,
An echo where two hearts attune.

With pies and laughter filling the air,
Unity found in the joy we share.
Each quip a bridge, each jest a cheer,
In echoes of unity, we draw near.

Beneath Our Shared Skies

Beneath the stars, we dream and grin,
Inventing tales of where we've been.
With silly stories that go awry,
We laugh till tears blur every eye.

From clouds that look like giant fries,
To rainbows made of pizza pies.
In whispered jokes and playful sighs,
We find the joy that never dies.

With each strange wish upon a star,
We know our bond will take us far.
Two goofy souls in cosmic play,
Beneath shared skies, we'll find our way.

In laughter's glow, we paint the night,
In every jest, we find our light.
Together, always, come what may,
In quirky joy, we'll dance and sway.

The Core of Connection

In coffee spills and jokes we tread,
With laughter spilled, our hearts are fed.
A nod, a wink, we know the game,
In silly strife, there's no true shame.

With puppy memes and cat-themed sighs,
We craft a laugh that never dies.
In every quirk, we find our spark,
With goofy antics, we light the dark.

The blender's song, our kitchen jam,
In messing up, we've made a plan.
To share the laughs, to mock the grind,
In every joke, true love we find.

So here's to us, in all we share,
A bond that thrives on silly care.
With every snort, we find perfection,
In this wild dance, the core's connection.

Mosaic of Memories

In this patchwork quilt of laughs,
We stitch our silly past,
With crayons, ice cream mustaches,
And epic wins that never last.

Sneaky pranks on sleepy heads,
Like dance moves in the rain,
We built our fortress from our joys,
What a wild, wacky gain!

Our photo albums filled with quirks,
Each snapshot tells a tale,
Of goofy hats and fishy grins,
In every detail, we prevail.

So here's to us, a merry crew,
With laughter as our glue,
In this grand mosaic we create,
Every moment feels brand new.

Intertwined Hearts

We dance like two left feet,
With mismatched socks and flair,
In this tangle of sweet chaos,
Who knew we'd make a pair?

Our hearts beat in a silly tune,
Like cats in a balloon,
When life hands us lemons, you see,
We juggle and we croon.

In the spice of our shared life,
We take the twists and turns,
With laughter as our guiding star,
In every fire, it burns.

So let's toast to quirky dreams,
And snort-laughing tight,
With intertwined hearts, we'll face the world,
In this playful delight.

The Pulse of Togetherness

We sync our joys and silly woes,
Like two koalas on a spree,
With goofy dances in our living room,
Our rhythm sets us free.

In this pulse we find our groove,
With moments quick and bright,
From pancake battles to pillow fights,
Every little spark ignites.

With coffee splashes and sock races,
We run through life's parade,
With chuckles echoing in the halls,
Together, never waylaid.

So who needs a grand plan, we say,
When laughter is our guide?
In this delightful symphony,
We embrace the joyful ride.

Unraveled Ties

Like noodles tangled on a plate,
Our lives twist and entwine,
With every slip and noodle knot,
We find the joy divine.

From misadventures to spilled juice,
We sail through our own tide,
Turning stumbles into stories,
With you right by my side.

Our bonds may twist like pretzels,
And twisty straws at best,
But in the end, it's pure delight,
In laughter, we invest.

So let's embrace the silly ties,
And relish in our ride,
With every joyful mishap, dear,
Our love can't be denied.

Luminous Paths

With socks that clash and don't quite match,
We dance through puddles, a funny patch.
Your laugh, a beacon, lights up the night,
As we trip on dreams, feeling just right.

In our mismatched world, we're quite the sight,
Like cats in tuxedos, a comical flight.
Running side by side, we gallop and sway,
In the glow of our quirks, we find our way.

Flickers of Togetherness

Your puns are clever, they come with a zing,
Like two silly birds, we humorously sing.
When you mime a duck, I burst out in glee,
Our laughter's a melody, just you and me.

From sneezing confetti to dancing around,
Each silly moment is joyfully found.
In this comedy show of friends turned to more,
We write our sketches, always wanting encore.

The Journey We Share

With backpacks stuffed and plans all askew,
Our map is a maze, but we'll find a view.
You call it a detour; I say it's a game,
In this wild adventure, it's never the same.

We'll ride a tandem bike, wobbly and fun,
With laughter echoing, we're never undone.
Through mishaps and giggles, our travels unfold,
Every stumble's a story, a memory retold.

Currents of Love

You spill your drink, I wear it with pride,
Our messy moments are joy multiplied.
Like two clumsy bears, we roll and we play,
In this playful chaos, we dance every day.

With jigsaw hearts that seem out of place,
We fit together in our own funny space.
In these waves of laughter that crash and refresh,
We find our rhythm, our bond, ever fresh.

Essence of Our Journey

In mismatched socks, we roam the streets,
With ice cream cones and dancing feet.
We laugh at maps all upside down,
Lost in the joy of our silly town.

With breadcrumbs left of pizza crust,
We've forged a trail in laughter's trust.
A compass spins, we make a bet,
The best adventures aren't found yet.

Kaleidoscope of Us

In swirling colors, we blend and break,
Like tangled yarn, we jiggle and shake.
A canvas bright, of dorky dreams,
We chuckle loud, or so it seems.

Each quirky laugh, a brushstroke cast,
In every moment, forever lasts.
With all our quirks, we dance and spin,
A crazy ride, let the fun begin!

Ties Beyond Time

With puns and jokes that never tire,
We hold our fate, a comical wire.
An inside joke, from years ago,
Keeps us together in the ebb and flow.

Through every flop and each sweet blunder,
We've slid on slips, yet never under.
Time's odd ties wrap tight and snug,
With laughter, we are forever bugged.

Soulful Navigation

In a sea of chaos, we sail with glee,
Maps in hand, our hearts run free.
A quirky crew of jokes afloat,
With punchlines written on a tiny boat.

Our GPS? It's giggles and grins,
Through wobbly waves, we rarely win.
But oh, dear friend, in the breezy fuss,
We steer our ship with joy—just us!

Soulful Entwining

In tangled socks, our dance begins,
We trip and laugh, it's where love wins.
Your hair's a nest, my hat's askew,
Together we're a whirling zoo.

We share our snacks and steal a bite,
You snore so loud, I lose the fight.
Your puns are bad, yet I still grin,
Together we lose, but always win.

Your quirks are bright, like neon lights,
We chase the moon on silly nights.
In every joke, a wink, a tease,
We float on clouds, with such great ease.

Through every mess, we find our groove,
In winding paths, we learn to move.
Our laughter rings like summer rain,
Entwined in joy, we dance again.

Radiant Bonds

Our selfies always come out weird,
With goofy faces, nothing's feared.
You stick your tongue out, I pull a face,
In this odd world, we find our place.

The neighbors laugh, they're in on the fun,
As we bring cupcakes, and eat each one.
You hide the frosting, I chase you down,
In this sweet game, you're the talk of the town.

With every chat and wobbly dance,
We take our leaps, we take our chance.
A world of hugs and silly rhymes,
In every moment, we conquer time.

Like mismatched socks, we're meant to be,
In this wild ride, you stay with me.
Our hearts are bold, our laughter bright,
In radiant bonds, we find delight.

The Fabric of Our Being

We weave our stories with silly string,
In every twist, a joy it brings.
You cut the thread, I stitch it back,
In this whole mess, we lose the track.

Your coffee spills, my tea goes cold,
In these small moments, warmth unfolds.
We play the game of "Did I say that?"
With comic timing, where's the cat?

Our trivia nights are pure farce,
You act like a clown, but still, I'll parse.
Through laughter shared and tears that flow,
In every stitch, our spirits grow.

The world's chaos can't break our seam,
In fabric bright, we live the dream.
With every laugh, we're sewing tight,
Bound together, we'll take flight.

Footprints in the Sand

We stroll along the beach with pride,
While stepping on crabs, we sometimes slide.
Your flip-flop flies, the seagulls cheer,
We laugh so loud, it's music here.

With sand in toes and hair a mess,
We build a castle, more or less.
It falls apart, but we don't mind,
In every flop, more joy we find.

The tide recedes, we chase the waves,
Like silly kids, we act like knaves.
You splash the water, I stand back,
In laughter filled, we lose the track.

Our footprints fade, but not our cheer,
Through every jest, you bring me near.
As sunset paints the sky so grand,
We leave our marks, hand in hand.

Imprints on Our Souls

In every laugh, a print appears,
Like pizza stains on borrowed chairs.
We gather stories, bold and bright,
With mismatched socks and sheer delight.

Like fingerprints in silly glue,
We stick together, just we two.
Through kitchen dance-offs, wild and loud,
Our hearts beat, silly, brave, and proud.

In coffee spills and fridge raids,
We craft our funny escapades.
With every quirk and playful tease,
We mark our place with such great ease.

So here's to us, the wacky team,
Chasing after every dream.
Through giggles shared under the sun,
Our silly journey's just begun.

Nexus of Experience

In the chaos of trying to cook,
We laugh at every recipe book.
With burnt toast and coffee spills,
We find joy in all our thrills.

Each mishap a tale for the ages,
Like wild actors tearing through stages.
With looks so silly, blunders galore,
Life's stage is fun, who could ask for more?

Like socks that vanish in the wash,
Our laughter is a joyful posh.
Through every scuffle and silly spat,
We dance like our favorite cat.

So here we blend, a funny brew,
In this wild world, just me and you.
Through epic fails and crazy quests,
Together we find our very best.

The Tapestry We Weave

With threads of joy, we spin our tale,
Like spunky squirrels on a rail.
Each stitch a laugh, each knot a hug,
We tuck in stories, cozy and snug.

Through quirky patterns and colorful schemes,
We weave together our wildest dreams.
With mismatched fabrics and buttons bright,
Our creation is pure delight.

In every twist, in every turn,
We gather wisdom — oh, how we learn!
With laughter loud and hearts so light,
We stitch our magic, day and night.

Together we're a vibrant mess,
In our tapestry, we find success.
With threads of whimsy and tales of cheer,
Here's to us, the darlings we hold dear.

Songs of Togetherness

In the chorus of our sweet refrain,
We laugh through sunshine and through rain.
With off-key notes and silly rhymes,
We dance like it's the best of times.

Every giggle a perfect beat,
Our melody, it can't be beat.
With crazy rhythms, we shake and sway,
Each moment a joyful cabaret.

From kitchen concerts to park parades,
We turn our life into charades.
With silly voices, we serenade,
In this duet, we're unafraid.

So let the world join in our song,
As we march through, dancing along.
With every laugh and joyful cheer,
Our harmony grows, year after year.

Pillars of Shared Joy

Laughter echoes in the air,
Sharing snacks without a care.
Silly jokes and funny faces,
In our world, we find our places.

Dancing like no one's around,
Socks just left on the ground.
We trip and fall, but who's to know?
Together we steal the show!

Bellyaches from laughter's toll,
You're the jelly to my roll.
With goofy antics, we ignite,
The spark of joy that feels so right.

Counting stars and munching pie,
Under a blanket of sky.
With every giggle, we ascend,
In this fun, we always blend.

Celestial Harmony

Like two planets in a spin,
Laughing loud over silly din.
Your quirks, a joyful mystery,
Together, we're a history.

We orbit round the goofy sun,
Chasing dreams, we've just begun.
In this dance of cosmic grace,
We find our rhythm, our own pace.

Asteroids made of cotton candy,
Comets slip by, feeling dandy.
In the galaxy of your smile,
We'll float on joy for a while.

Time's a prankster, playing tricks,
But our laughs can bridge the mix.
In this universe so wide,
You're my laughter, my dear guide.

Whispers of Our Togetherness

In whispers soft, we share our jokes,
Joining in with the funniest folks.
With eyes that twinkle, we create,
A world of laughter, truly great.

Bubble baths and rubber ducks,
Inviting giggles, not bad lucks.
As we splash and splash away,
It's joy that colors our day.

Our little secrets, peculiar quirks,
In every word, the mischief lurks.
We trade our stories 'round the fire,
With laughter, we never tire.

Each moment shared is a pure delight,
You're my favorite, day and night.
With every chuckle, our bond grows strong,
In this funny dance, we belong!

Threads of Shared Existence

Through tangled threads, we weave our fate,
Silly antics, never late.
With each stitch, a laugh is sewn,
In this fabric, we have grown.

Patchwork hearts, we craft with glee,
Every bump is a jubilee.
Our colors blend in crazy ways,
Turning mundane into bright days.

Napping under the quilt of dreams,
Life's fun in the silliest schemes.
Each little mess, a tale we share,
In this tapestry, love is rare.

With every brother-in-arms whim,
Our shared existence, a joyful hymn.
So let's stitch the world with cheer,
Forever and always, I'm glad you're near.

Whispers of Togetherness

In a kitchen dance, we trip and twirl,
Spilling pasta as laughter unfurls.
Your socks are mismatched, a colorful sight,
Still, you claim you dress with pure delight.

The cat's a witness, a silent judge,
As we argue who's turn it is to budge.
Popcorn fights during a movie night,
You scream at the screen, I just delight.

Pretzels in hand, we play silly games,
Painter's tape, and ridiculous names.
Your victory dance is quite the show,
While I plot my revenge for the next round, though!

But in all these quirks, our bond shines bright,
In a chaotic world, we're each other's light.
With snorts and snickers, our hearts align,
In the jest of life, you're forever mine.

Threads of Connection

You wear my sweater, it stretches wide,
I've never seen such a fashion ride!
We take silly selfies, making faces galore,
Each click a memory, and laughter by score.

Your coffee spills, I roll my eyes,
Yet, it's those moments that are the prize.
Pajama days with a blanket fort,
We're the kings and queens of our quirky court.

Oh, the secrets shared whisper low,
Jokes coded in laughter, only we know.
A noodle fight in the kitchen's embrace,
No fancy restaurant can match our grace.

With every blooper, our giggles stack,
Like mismatched socks in an old backpack.
Through life's tapestry, we weave and play,
In the fabric of joy, don't fade away.

Echoes of Our Being

In the silence, your snoring's a song,
A symphony, though often quite wrong.
Midnight snacks become a secret quest,
We raid the fridge, and it's always a fest!

Your puns are terrible, but I love them still,
A comedy act that gives me a thrill.
The blanket war's on, I take my stand,
But you sneak in to claim your land.

We chase the sunset, hand in hand,
But trip on shadows, isn't it grand?
Dancing like dorks in the pale moonlight,
We laugh at the world, making it bright.

As we tumble through life, quirky and bold,
In laughter's embrace, our stories unfold.
Through echoes of moments, together we sing,
Finding joy in the chaos, that's our thing.

Heartbeats in Harmony

In rhythm and rhyme, we stumble and sway,
Your two left feet lead the dance away.
With shared ice cream, we create a mess,
Sticky fingers, yet I must confess.

You steal my fries, and I raise an eyebrow,
It's a tiny battle in our shared vow.
Whispers of secrets, silly and sweet,
In the playful dance of our heartbeat's beat.

We build a fortress of pillows and dreams,
Two grown-up kids, or so it seems.
Jokes on the breeze, as the clock strikes one,
In the game of life, it's all just for fun.

Sprinkling love in the quirks and the flaws,
With every adventure, we pause for applause.
Through heartbeats in harmony, we shall glide,
In the laughter of moments, forever we bide.

Echoing Hearts

We laughed at clouds, so round and puffy,
Chasing rainbows that looked a bit fluffy.
In random dances, our shadows twirl,
A silly game, just us in this whirl.

We spilled our secrets to a friendly cat,
Who nodded wisely, a furry diplomat.
With giggles echoing, we shared our snacks,
Two goofy hearts, no room for lacks.

We wear mismatched socks, it's quite the trend,
Every day's just another silly blend.
In a world of chaos, we find our way,
With laughter leading us, hip-hip-hooray!

So here's our anthem: let's laugh and sing,
In our little kingdom, we're the quirky king.
This joyous bond, like bubbles, will float,
Forever together, we'll never gloat.

Spirals of Intimacy

We twist like spaghetti, a dance so fine,
Spilling some sauce with our silly line.
Your laugh's a melody, a quirky tune,
Like socks in the dryer, we spin, we swoon.

In puddles we jump, like kids with no care,
Who needs an umbrella? We'll splash and share!
With chocolate on fingers, we made our mark,
Life's a sweet treat, igniting the spark.

Our silly selfies, with faces so grim,
Caught in this vortex, we take a swim.
Through funhouse mirrors, we see the jest,
In twisted reflections, we're truly blessed.

So let's paint the town with our joy divine,
In this wild dance, our hearts entwine.
No script to follow, just laughter and glee,
In our quirky world, we are always free.

Ribbons of Shared Dreams

We tied our hopes with ribbons of flair,
Each wish a balloon, floating up in air.
In the kitchen chaos, the flour flies high,
With dough on our noses, we bake pies on the fly.

Our dreams like kittens, chasing a beam,
Tangled together, like a wild stream.
We built a fort from cushions and sheets,
And declared it's home, with our favorite treats.

We share "secrets" sipped from sippy cups,
Exchanging our laughter like joyful hiccups.
With playful banter and quirks on parade,
This carnival life is beautifully made.

So let's ride this wave, on laughter we surf,
Our goofy adventures, they brighten the earth.
Together we'll bask in our whimsical beams,
For life's just a canvas, filled with our dreams.

Unity in Diversity

We dance to the beat of our mismatched shoes,
With a dash of chaos, we simply can't lose.
In our patchwork lives, every color shines,
Together we're rich, with spaghetti lines.

You're sweet like candy; I'm spicy like curry,
In our playful kitchen, there's never a hurry.
We mix up our flavors, then sit and feast,
Every bite a laughter, a love released.

Our quirks are the threads in this fabric spun,
Diverse but united—we laugh, we run.
Like a circus parade on an uncharted spree,
Together we flourish, like a wild honeybee.

So let's grab the world in our goofy embrace,
With laughter and love, the silly will grace.
In this jumbled journey, we're the perfect pair,
This whimsical friendship, beyond any compare.

The Glow of Together

In a world of chaos, we dance and spin,
Two quirky souls, let the laughter begin.
You steal my fries, I borrow your hat,
Together we're silly, imagine that!

With every mistake, we giggle aloud,
Dancing like fools, so crazy, so proud.
You trip on the rug, I spill my drink,
But in our mischief, we never rethink.

Our inside jokes, stitched tight in our hearts,
Like socks on a ceiling, true work of art.
We paint silly faces on clouds in the sky,
With you by my side, oh me, oh my!

So here's to the moments, both big and small,
The slip-ups and punchlines, we cherish them all.
With giggles and grins, we'll weather the fuss,
In this colorful circus, just me and you thus!

Elements of Our Story

We're like peanut butter, and jelly, oh yes,
A mix of sweet chaos, your favorite mess.
With socks that don't match and hair out of whack,
Our blend of oddities, there's never a lack!

You dance like a chicken, I sing like a frog,
In the tales that we tell, we're one goofy cog.
Late-night snacks and funny cat memes,
Together we're bursting at the seams!

From pancake flips to the ice cream fight,
We've conquered our fears, turned wrongs into right.
With a sprinkle of chaos and a splash of fun,
Our journey rolls on, it's just begun!

So side by side, let the laughter resound,
In this funny tale, joy is always found.
With every mishap, we build our legacy,
Through giggles and quirks, the best company!

Lifelines Intertwined

In a world of tangled strings,
We laugh at all our flings.
Your sock's on my foot, it's quite a sight,
Together we bumble, oh what a delight!

Grocery lists that make no sense,
We argue over pizza or dense expense.
Yet in the chaos, joy is found,
In silly moments, laughter's profound.

You trip on air, I spill my tea,
Our dance of clumsiness, just you and me.
We share our quirks like secret codes,
Life's little jokes lighten our loads.

Unraveled threads, we weave anew,
In this tapestry, it's just us two.
Woven with giggles, stitched with cheer,
Forever entwined, that's perfectly clear.

Starlit Companionship

Underneath the winking skies,
I poke you, you roll your eyes.
Your goofy grin, a cosmic show,
We dance in moonlight, soft and slow.

You steal the blankets, I claim the bed,
Who knew such battles could leave us wed?
Laughing as we wrestle for warmth and space,
Your ridiculous snoring that I can't outpace.

A meteor shower of laughter bright,
We count our wishes, what a sight!
Pizza slices and dreams collide,
In this silly tale, we take odd pride.

Together we shine, two stars in flight,
Navigating through the jokes of the night.
Your laugh's the music I want to hear,
In this starlit dance, I'm glad you're near.

Shadows of Our Truth

In shadows deep, we crack a joke,
Finding giggles where others choke.
Your silly dance makes the sun peek through,
In our wonky world, it's just me and you.

We build a castle from our dreams,
With cardboard fortresses, laugh 'til we scream.
Pointless debates on whose turn to play,
In this wacky ream, we always stay.

Your awkward twirl, my wildhair spree,
Together we're as funny as can be.
Every moment's a sitcom, a sketch, a play,
Chasing shadows in our own silly way.

Through ups and downs, we navigate,
Finding delight in the most mundane state.
In the shadows where our laughter thrives,
We're the comedians of our wild lives!

Embrace of the Infinite

In a hug that's far too tight,
We laugh as we fight for elbow light.
Each twist and turn, a shared routine,
Your goofy smile shines like a queen.

We spin like tops, heads in a whirl,
Your hair's a nest—what a wild curl!
Yet in this chaos, we find our way,
A funny dance that ends the day.

With every step, we trip and fall,
Yet rise with giggles, love's final call.
Through slip-ups and snorts, we navigate,
In this infinite hug, we're truly great!

Each quirk and laugh, our masterpiece,
In the frame of silly, we find our peace.
Together we're weird, yes, that's true,
In the embrace of the infinite, it's just me and you.

Our Unique Symphony

In a world of quirks and laughs,
We dance to beats of silly drafts,
With every note, we share a grin,
A tune so bright, we can't keep in.

We sing off-key, yet still in tune,
Like cats that howl beneath the moon,
Each harmony, a joyful mess,
A laughter track, no need to stress.

A trumpet's honk, a tambourine,
Our orchestra of garlic beans,
With every laugh, a different sound,
Together in this joy we're bound.

Each quirk a note, each joke a smile,
We'll turn our everyday to style,
In this unique, hilarious song,
We find our place where we belong.

Streams of Shared Energy

Like coffee beans, we brew and blend,
Electric sparks, around the bend,
With every joke, we boost the charge,
Our giggles echo, loud and large.

We zap and zoom in giddy flight,
Our banter shakes the stars at night,
With jolly jests and playful pranks,
We fill our sails with laughter's thanks.

A stream of fun, it flows and bends,
Through funny quirks, our journey sends,
In every smile, a current flows,
Together we ignite, who knows?

We surf the waves of silly schemes,
Creating laughter from our dreams,
This power's ours, a funny flood,
In every drip, we find the love.

The Pulse Beneath the Surface

A giggle thrum beneath the skin,
A secret beat, let laughter in,
With every chuckle, we feel the rhythm,
This pulse of joy, it's ours to give 'em.

A thump, a bump, a pun on cue,
We groove together, me and you,
In every jest, a heartbeat shared,
Our funny dance, we've always dared.

In dance of words, we start to sway,
With silly songs, we break the gray,
Our playful jig, like bunny hops,
In rhythm found, the laughter pops.

A hidden pulse, it guides us through,
In each soft smile, we find the clue,
For life's a beat, we make it ours,
In giggles spun, we find our powers.

Ripples of Knowing

In every chuckle shared with you,
A ripple spreads, as good friends do,
We toss our jokes like rocks in streams,
Creating waves in laughter's dreams.

We know the tune of silly sights,
In bursts of joy, we spark delights,
With every pun, the ripples play,
Reflecting joy, our own ballet.

A wave of laughter, it flows with grace,
In every grin, we find our space,
As quips bounce back like boomerangs,
Our joy erupts in silly flangs.

In ripples wide, we softly tread,
With every joke, new paths we thread,
This dance of laughter, pure and bright,
Reflects the bond we hold so tight.

Radiance of Togetherness

In a world of mismatched socks,
We dance in our silly crocs.
Fumbling with spaghetti twirls,
Our laughter fuels the swirls.

You tell jokes that go astray,
I throw my head back and sway.
Lost in tangents, oh what fun,
Together we shine like the sun.

At picnics, ants join our feast,
You say they're just party beasts.
I'm sure they laugh at our game,
In our chaos, they find fame.

Through life's mess, there's art to see,
With you, I'm blissfully free.
So let's keep our quirks in parade,
In this laughter, we're unafraid.

Harmony in Dissonance

Our karaoke skills are rare,
Kittens run when they hear our flair.
You belt high notes, I hit the floor,
Together, we're one glorious bore.

Making pancakes turns into wars,
Flour fights break out with roars.
Sticky syrup on the wall,
History says we had a ball.

With mismatched tunes, we shall sing,
A cacophony of joy we bring.
You step on toes, I start to glide,
In our jumbled dance, we find pride.

In our clash, we create delight,
Like fireworks igniting the night.
So here's to our funny charade,
In this symphony, we've made.

Portrait of Existence

Did you just paint the cat blue?
Artistic flair, that much is true.
With crayons, we sketch our days,
In scribbles and messy ways.

Our coffee cups spill with grace,
Meeting chaos face to face.
Brushes dipped in laughter's hue,
Life's canvas is meant for two.

We create memes of daily strife,
Documenting our silly life.
With every blunder, smiles grow wide,
In this portrait, love won't hide.

Collages of our wacky ways,
Make each moment worth the gaze.
In this gallery of delight,
We laugh together, day and night.

Alchemy of Love

With potions brewed in mismatched mugs,
We mix joy and silly hugs.
Your charm is like garlic bread,
Served hot and slathered, that's how it's fed.

We're scientists of giggles and glee,
Creating compounds, just you and me.
Bubbling laughter fills the air,
In our lab, there's love everywhere.

Our experiments often go wrong,
But we always end up strong.
A sprinkle of quirks and a dash of play,
Turns dull moments into a ballet.

So here's to our crazy concoction,
Life's recipe needs no reduction.
With fun in each beaker we share,
In this alchemy, love is rare.

Vibrations in the Void

In the silence, we dance, so spry,
Our laughter echoes, reaching the sky.
With quirky moves, we swing and sway,
The universe giggles, come what may.

When the stars align, we bounce around,
In silly rhythms, joy is found.
Gravity's pull can't keep us still,
With each silly jig, we heighten the thrill.

A wobbly twirl, a goofy grin,
In this wild void, we both win.
Even black holes chuckle at our play,
As we hop through space in a wacky way.

So let's strut in this cosmic show,
With our quirks and quirks the galactic glow.
When the void sings, we jump on cue,
In the dance of life, it's me and you.

Within Each Other's Light

She shines like a star, bright and bold,
With laughter so loud, it's pure gold.
I'm her shadow, forever in tow,
In the glow of her humor, my heart's aglow.

We joke about aliens, their bad style,
In each other's light, we bask for a while.
Her puns hit harder than a comet's chase,
As we float in the waves of our own space.

When shadows grow long, we're a quirky team,
Creating a world from the silliest dream.
In the warmth of our giggles, joy takes flight,
Finding wonder within each other's light.

So here's to the moments, bright and cheap,
In our universe, the joy runs deep.
With our sparkles and quirks, we're never apart,
Laughing together, you illuminate my heart.

Garden of Us

In a garden where laughter blooms bright,
We plant little jokes, morning to night.
With every giggle, a flower sprouts,
In this patch of hilarity, joy never doubts.

A sunflower smiles, it knows we're near,
Waving its petals, big and clear.
While daisies giggle at our silly chats,
We dance with the sprigs and twirl with the mats.

We water our dreams with hearty gleams,
Pulling weeds of worry, sharing our schemes.
The fruits of our humor, ripe and sweet,
In this garden, life just can't be beat.

So let's grow wild, no time to fuss,
In the soil of friendship, it's just us.
With laughter as sunshine, we'll always trust,
In the magic we share, in the garden of us.

Aromas of Affection

In the kitchen, we stir and swirl,
With spices and giggles, our flavors twirl.
A dash of laughter, a pinch of fun,
Cooking together, we're never outdone.

The aroma of garlic, the sizzle and pop,
Each meal a circus, we just can't stop.
Her cookies are jokes, sweet with a dash,
While my soup's a comedy hit, oh what a clash!

We season our lives with humorous zest,
In this culinary quest, we never rest.
As smiles rise like bread, fresh and warm,
Aromas of laughter keep us in form.

So here's to the dishes we serve with a cheer,
With each silly bite, love drops near.
In our kitchen of joy, flavors combust,
Creating a feast, it's an aromatic trust.

9 789908 010731